Personal Information

Name: _____

Address: _____ Postcode: _____

Telephone: _____ Mobi' _____

Email: _____

GW00514926

2025

JANUARY						
S	M	T	W	T	F	S
			1	2	3	4
5	6	7	8	9	10	11
12	13	14	15	16	17	18
19	20	21	22	23	24	25
26	27	28	29	30	31	

FEBRUARY						
S	M	T	W	T	F	S
						1
2	3	4	5	6	7	8
9	10	11	12	13	14	15
16	17	18	19	20	21	22
23	24	25	26	27	28	

MARCH						
S	M	T	W	T	F	S
30	31					1
2	3	4	5	6	7	8
9	10	11	12	13	14	15
16	17	18	19	20	21	22
23	24	25	26	27	28	29

APRIL						
S	M	T	W	T	F	S
		1	2	3	4	5
6	7	8	9	10	11	12
13	14	15	16	17	18	19
20	21	22	23	24	25	26
27	28	29	30			

MAY						
S	M	T	W	T	F	S
				1	2	3
4	5	6	7	8	9	10
11	12	13	14	15	16	17
18	19	20	21	22	23	24
25	26	27	28	29	30	31

JUNE						
S	M	T	W	T	F	S
1	2	3	4	5	6	7
8	9	10	11	12	13	14
15	16	17	18	19	20	21
22	23	24	25	26	27	28
29	30					

JULY						
S	M	T	W	T	F	S
		1	2	3	4	5
6	7	8	9	10	11	12
13	14	15	16	17	18	19
20	21	22	23	24	25	26
27	28	29	30	31		

AUGUST						
S	M	T	W	T	F	S
31					1	2
3	4	5	6	7	8	9
10	11	12	13	14	15	16
17	18	19	20	21	22	23
24	25	26	27	28	29	30

SEPTEMBER						
S	M	T	W	T	F	S
	1	2	3	4	5	6
7	8	9	10	11	12	13
14	15	16	17	18	19	20
21	22	23	24	25	26	27
28	29	30				

OCTOBER						
S	M	T	W	T	F	S
			1	2	3	4
5	6	7	8	9	10	11
12	13	14	15	16	17	18
19	20	21	22	23	24	25
26	27	28	29	30	31	

NOVEMBER						
S	M	T	W	T	F	S
30						1
2	3	4	5	6	7	8
9	10	11	12	13	14	15
16	17	18	19	20	21	22
23	24	25	26	27	28	29

DECEMBER						
S	M	T	W	T	F	S
	1	2	3	4	5	6
7	8	9	10	11	12	13
14	15	16	17	18	19	20
21	22	23	24	25	26	27
28	29	30	31			

Fading light on Thistle Cove, Cape Le Grand National Park, Western Australia.

Wild Places

2025 Year Planner

	JANUARY	FEBRUARY	MARCH	APRIL	MAY	JUNE
SUN			31			1
MON						2
TUE				1		3
WED	1			2		4
THU	2			3	1	5
FRI	3			4	2	6
SAT	4	1	1	5	3	7
SUN	5	2	2	6	4	8
MON	6	3	3	7	5	9
TUE	7	4	4	8	6	10
WED	8	5	5	9	7	11
THU	9	6	6	10	8	12
FRI	10	7	7	11	9	13
SAT	11	8	8	12	10	14
SUN	12	9	9	13	11	15
MON	13	10	10	14	12	16
TUE	14	11	11	15	13	17
WED	15	12	12	16	14	18
THU	16	13	13	17	15	19
FRI	17	14	14	18	16	20
SAT	18	15	15	19	17	21
SUN	19	16	16	20	18	22
MON	20	17	17	21	19	23
TUE	21	18	18	22	20	24
WED	22	19	19	23	21	25
THU	23	20	20	24	22	26
FRI	24	21	21	25	23	27
SAT	25	22	22	26	24	28
SUN	26	23	23	27	25	29
MON	27	24	24	28	26	30
TUE	28	25	25	29	27	
WED	29	26	26	30	28	
THU	30	27	27		29	
FRI	31	28	28		30	
SAT			29		31	
SUN			30			

	JULY	AUGUST	SEPTEMBER	OCTOBER	NOVEMBER	DECEMBER
SUN						
MON			1			1
TUE	1		2			2
WED	2		3	1		3
THU	3		4	2		4
FRI	4	1	5	3		5
SAT	5	2	6	4	1	6
SUN	6	3	7	5	2	7
MON	7	4	8	6	3	8
TUE	8	5	9	7	4	9
WED	9	6	10	8	5	10
THU	10	7	11	9	6	11
FRI	11	8	12	10	7	12
SAT	12	9	13	11	8	13
SUN	13	10	14	12	9	14
MON	14	11	15	13	10	15
TUE	15	12	16	14	11	16
WED	16	13	17	15	12	17
THU	17	14	18	16	13	18
FRI	18	15	19	17	14	19
SAT	19	16	20	18	15	20
SUN	20	17	21	19	16	21
MON	21	18	22	20	17	22
TUE	22	19	23	21	18	23
WED	23	20	24	22	19	24
THU	24	21	25	23	20	25
FRI	25	22	26	24	21	26
SAT	26	23	27	25	22	27
SUN	27	24	28	26	23	28
MON	28	25	29	27	24	29
TUE	29	26	30	28	25	30
WED	30	27		29	26	31
THU	31	28		30	27	
FRI		29		31	28	
SAT		30			29	
SUN		31			30	

Public Holidays

National

New Year's Day	Wednesday 1 January
Australia Day/Survivor's Day	Sunday 26 January**
Australia Day Holiday	Monday 27 January
Good Friday	Friday 18 April
Easter Saturday	Saturday 19 April
Easter Sunday	Sunday 20 April
Easter Monday	Monday 21 April
Anzac Day	Friday 25 April
Kings's Birthday (except Qld & WA)	Monday 9 June
Christmas Day	Thursday 25 December
Boxing Day	Friday 26 December

Australian Capital Territory

Canberra Day	Monday 10 March
Reconciliation Day Holiday	Monday 2 June
Labour Day	Monday 6 October

New South Wales

Labour Day	Monday 6 October

Northern Territory

May Day	Monday 5 May
Picnic Day	Monday 4 August

Queensland

Labour Day	Monday 5 May
Brisbane Show Day	Wednesday 13 August*
King's Birthday	Monday 6 October

South Australia

Adelaide Cup Day	Monday 10 March
Labour Day	Monday 6 October

Tasmania

Royal Hobart Regatta	Monday 10 February*
Eight Hours Day	Monday 10 March
Easter Tuesday	Tuesday 22 April*
Royal Hobart Show Day	Thursday 23 October*
Recreation Day	Monday 3 November*

Victoria

Labour Day	Monday 10 March
Melbourne Cup Day	Tuesday 4 November

Western Australia

Labour Day	Monday 3 March
Western Australia Day	Monday 2 June
King's Birthday	Monday 29 September

*Regionally observed or subject to state specific conditions.
**Date subject to change.

The information listed on this page has been gathered from various sources. Steven Nowakowski Publishing has taken all care in compiling this information, however no responsibility is taken for the accuracy of the information and readers are advised to make their own enquiries regarding the dates listed above.

Holiday and school dates are subject to change by authorities. Information correct at 1 February 2024.

School Terms 2025

Australian Capital Territory

Term 1	3 February – 11 April
Term 2	29 April – 4 July
Term 3	22 July – 26 September
Term 4	14 October – 18 December

New South Wales

Term 1	31 January – 11 April (Eastern)
	7 February – 11 April (Western)
Term 2	28 April – 4 July
Term 3	21 July – 26 September
Term 4	13 October – 19 December

Northern Territory

Term 1	29 January – 4 April
Term 2	14 April – 20 June
Term 3	15 July – 19 September
Term 4	6 October – 12 December

Queensland

Term 1	28 January – 4 April
Term 2	22 April – 27 June
Term 3	14 July – 19 September
Term 4	7 October – 12 December

South Australia

Term 1	28 January – 11 April
Term 2	28 April – 4 July
Term 3	21 July – 26 September
Term 4	13 October – 12 December

Tasmania

Term 1	6 February – 11 April
Term 2	28 April – 4 July
Term 3	21 July – 26 September
Term 4	13 October – 18 December

Victoria

Term 1	29 January – 4 April
Term 2	22 April – 4 July
Term 3	21 July – 19 September
Term 4	6 October – 19 December

Western Australia

Term 1	5 February – 11 April
Term 2	28 April – 4 July
Term 3	21 July – 26 September
Term 4	13 October – 18 December

Photograph Locations
Listed by week

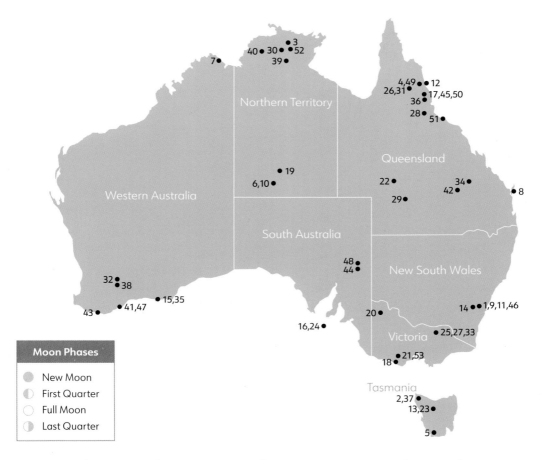

Astrological Signs, Elements and Birthstones

MONTH	ASTROLOGICAL SIGN	BIRTHSTONE
22 Dec – 19 Jan	Capricorn (earth)	Garnet (January)
20 Jan – 18 Feb	Aquarius (air)	Amethyst (February)
19 Feb – 20 Mar	Pisces (water)	Aquamarine (March)
21 Mar – 19 Apr	Aries (fire)	Diamond (April)
20 Apr – 20 May	Taurus (earth)	Emerald (May)
21 May – 21 Jun	Gemini (air)	Pearl (June)
22 Jun – 22 Jul	Cancer (water)	Ruby (July)
23 Jul – 22 Aug	Leo (fire)	Peridot (August)
23 Aug – 22 Sep	Virgo (earth)	Sapphire (September)
23 Sep – 22 Oct	Libra (air)	Opal (October)
23 Oct – 21 Nov	Scorpio (water)	Topaz (November)
22 Nov – 21 Dec	Sagittarius (fire)	Turquoise (December)

Early morning mist rising from Jamison Valley,
Blue Mountains National Park, New South Wales.

Week 1

December / January

30 monday

31 tuesday

1 wednesday   New Year's Day

2 thursday

3 friday

4 saturday

5 sunday

			JANUARY			
S	M	T	W	T	F	S
				1	2	3	4
5	6	7	8	9	10	11
12	13	14	15	16	17	18
19	20	21	22	23	24	25
26	27	28	29	30	31	

Flourishing fungi in Trowutta Arch State Reserve,
Tarkine region, Tasmania.

Week 2

6 monday

_____

_____

_____

7 tuesday ◑

_____

_____

_____

8 wednesday

_____

_____

_____

9 thursday

_____

_____

_____

10 friday

_____

_____

_____

11 saturday

_____

_____

_____

12 sunday

_____

_____

JANUARY

S	M	T	W	T	F	S
				1	2	3	4
5	6	7	8	9	10	11
12	13	14	15	16	17	18
19	20	21	22	23	24	25
26	27	28	29	30	31	

Wet season build up, Kakadu National Park, Northern Territiory.
Photo: Stanley Breeden.

Week 3

13 monday

14 tuesday ○

15 wednesday

16 thursday

17 friday

18 saturday

19 sunday

JANUARY

S	M	T	W	T	F	S
			1	2	3	4
5	6	7	8	9	10	11
12	13	14	15	16	17	18
19	20	21	22	23	24	25
26	27	28	29	30	31	

The lace work canopy of the Wooroonooran teatree *(Leptospermum wooroonooran)*, Mount Lewis National Park, Queensland.

Week 4

January

20 monday
_____
_____

21 tuesday
_____
_____

22 wednesday ◑
_____
_____

23 thursday
_____
_____

24 friday
_____
_____

25 saturday
_____
_____

26 sunday   Australia Day
              Survivor's Day
_____

JANUARY

S	M	T	W	T	F	S
				1	2	3	4
5	6	7	8	9	10	11
12	13	14	15	16	17	18
19	20	21	22	23	24	25
26	27	28	29	30	31	

Reflections across a calm Bathurst Harbour with Mt Rugby in distance,
Southwest National Park, Tasmania.

Week 5

January / February

27 monday   Australia Day Holiday

28 tuesday

29 wednesday ●

30 thursday

31 friday

1 saturday

2 sunday

FEBRUARY						
S	M	T	W	T	F	S
						1
2	3	4	5	6	7	8
9	10	11	12	13	14	15
16	17	18	19	20	21	22
23	24	25	26	27	28	

Seasonal rainfall cascading down Uluru-Kata Tjuta near Mutitjulu
Waterhole, Uluru-Kata Tjuta National Park, Northern Territory.
Photo: Stanley Breeden

Week 6

3 monday

4 tuesday

5 wednesday ◑

6 thursday Waitangi Day (NZ)

7 friday

8 saturday

9 sunday

FEBRUARY						
S	M	T	W	T	F	S
						1
2	3	4	5	6	7	8
9	10	11	12	13	14	15
16	17	18	19	20	21	22
23	24	25	26	27	28	

Weathered rock pavements at Wollangooyoo Pool,
Kimberley Region, Western Australia.
Photo: Kerry Trapnell.

Week 7

10 monday   Royal Hobart Regatta (Tas)

_____

_____

_____

11 tuesday

_____

_____

_____

12 wednesday

_____

_____

_____

13 thursday ○

_____

_____

_____

14 friday   Valentine's Day

_____

_____

_____

15 saturday

_____

_____

_____

16 sunday

_____

_____

_____

FEBRUARY

S	M	T	W	T	F	S
						1
2	3	4	5	6	7	8
9	10	11	12	13	14	15
16	17	18	19	20	21	22
23	24	25	26	27	28	

Crystal clear waters of Wanggoolba Creek, K'gari,
Great Sandy National Park, Queensland.

Week 8

17 monday

18 tuesday

19 wednesday

20 thursday

21 friday ◑

22 saturday

23 sunday

FEBRUARY

S	M	T	W	T	F	S
						1
2	3	4	5	6	7	8
9	10	11	12	13	14	15
16	17	18	19	20	21	22
23	24	25	26	27	28	

Sheer sandstone escarpments of Burramoko Ridge (Hanging Rock)
in Blue Mountains National Park, New South Wales.

Week 9

24 monday

25 tuesday

26 wednesday

27 thursday

28 friday ●

1 saturday

2 sunday

MARCH						
S	M	T	W	T	F	S
30	31					1
2	3	4	5	6	7	8
9	10	11	12	13	14	15
16	17	18	19	20	21	22
23	24	25	26	27	28	29

A drifting rain squall over Uluru-Kata Tjuta National Park,
Northern Territory.
Photo: Stanley Breeden.

Week 10

3 monday   Labour Day (WA)

4 tuesday

5 wednesday

6 thursday

7 friday ◑

8 saturday

9 sunday

MARCH

S	M	T	W	T	F	S
30	31					1
2	3	4	5	6	7	8
9	10	11	12	13	14	15
16	17	18	19	20	21	22
23	24	25	26	27	28	29

Flannel flower *(Actinotus helianthi)*, Blue Mountains National Park,
New South Wales.

Week 11

March

10 monday   Labour Day (Vic), Eight Hours Day (Tas), Adelaide Cup Day (SA), Canberra Day (ACT)

11 tuesday

12 wednesday

13 thursday

14 friday ○

15 saturday

16 sunday

MARCH						
S	M	T	W	T	F	S
30	31					1
2	3	4	5	6	7	8
9	10	11	12	13	14	15
16	17	18	19	20	21	22
23	24	25	26	27	28	29

Elegant fan palms *(Licuala Ramsayii)* deep in the heart of the lowland
Daintree rainforest, Daintree National Park, Queensland.

Week 12

17 monday   St Patrick's Day

18 tuesday

19 wednesday

20 thursday

21 friday   Harmony Day

22 saturday ☽

23 sunday

MARCH

S	M	T	W	T	F	S
30	31					1
2	3	4	5	6	7	8
9	10	11	12	13	14	15
16	17	18	19	20	21	22
23	24	25	26	27	28	29

Glacial tarn with towering West Wall beyond,
Walls of Jerusalem National Park, Tasmania.

Week 13

24 monday

25 tuesday

26 wednesday

27 thursday

28 friday

29 saturday ●

30 sunday

MARCH

S	M	T	W	T	F	S
30	31					1
2	3	4	5	6	7	8
9	10	11	12	13	14	15
16	17	18	19	20	21	22
23	24	25	26	27	28	29

Greater glider *(Petauroides volans)* in eucalypt forest near Oberon
that has now been clear felled for pine plantations, New South Wales.
Photo: Stanley Breeden.

Week 14

31 monday

1 tuesday

2 wednesday

3 thursday

4 friday

5 saturday ◑

6 sunday

			APRIL			
S	**M**	**T**	**W**	**T**	**F**	**S**
		1	2	3	4	5
6	7	8	9	10	11	12
13	14	15	16	17	18	19
20	21	22	23	24	25	26
27	28	29	30			

Rock monolith overlooking Thistle Cove, Cape Le Grand National Park, Western Australia.

Week 15

7 monday

8 tuesday

9 wednesday

10 thursday

11 friday

12 saturday

13 sunday ○

			APRIL			
S	M	T	W	T	F	S
		1	2	3	4	5
6	7	8	9	10	11	12
13	14	15	16	17	18	19
20	21	22	23	24	25	26
27	28	29	30			

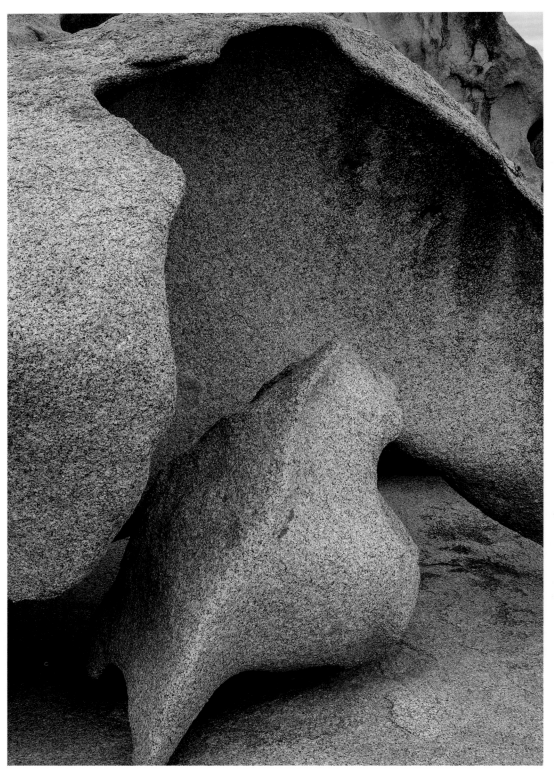

Wind worn and algae encrusted Remarkable Rocks,
Flinders Chase National Park, South Australia.

Week 16

14 monday

15 tuesday

16 wednesday

17 thursday

18 friday   Good Friday

19 saturday   Easter Saturday

20 sunday   Easter Sunday

APRIL

S	M	T	W	T	F	S
		1	2	3	4	5
6	7	8	9	10	11	12
13	14	15	16	17	18	19
20	21	22	23	24	25	26
27	28	29	30			

A tributary of the Russell River, Wooroonooran National Park, Queensland.

Week 17

21 monday   ◑ Easter Monday

22 tuesday   Easter Tuesday (Tas)

23 wednesday

24 thursday

25 friday   Anzac Day

26 saturday

27 sunday

			APRIL			
S	M	T	W	T	F	S
		1	2	3	4	5
6	7	8	9	10	11	12
13	14	15	16	17	18	19
20	21	22	23	24	25	26
27	28	29	30			

Shifting tides along the coastline of
Twelve Apostles Marine National Park, Victoria.

Week 18

28 monday ●

29 tuesday

30 wednesday

1 thursday

2 friday

3 saturday

4 sunday ◑

MAY						
S	M	T	W	T	F	S
					1	2	3
4	5	6	7	8	9	10
11	12	13	14	15	16	17
18	19	20	21	22	23	24
25	26	27	28	29	30	31

The highest peak in the Northern Territory rises above the
vast eroded landscape of Tjoritja/West MacDonnell National Park,
Northern Territory.

Week 19

5 monday May Day (NT)
Labour Day (Qld)

6 tuesday

7 wednesday

8 thursday

9 friday

10 saturday

11 sunday Mother's Day

MAY

S	M	T	W	T	F	S
				1	2	3
4	5	6	7	8	9	10
11	12	13	14	15	16	17
18	19	20	21	22	23	24
25	26	27	28	29	30	31

Pink cockatoo *(Lophochroa leadbeateri)*,
Murray-Sunset National Park, Victoria.
Photo: D Parer & E Parer-Cook.

Week 20

12 monday

13 tuesday ○

14 wednesday

15 thursday

16 friday

17 saturday

18 sunday

MAY						
S	M	T	W	T	F	S
				1	2	3
4	5	6	7	8	9	10
11	12	13	14	15	16	17
18	19	20	21	22	23	24
25	26	27	28	29	30	31

Myrtle beech *(Nothofagus cunninghamii)*, Aire River,
Great Otway National Park, Victoria

Week 21

19 monday

20 tuesday ◑

21 wednesday

22 thursday

23 friday

24 saturday

25 sunday

MAY						
S	M	T	W	T	F	S
				1	2	3
4	5	6	7	8	9	10
11	12	13	14	15	16	17
18	19	20	21	22	23	24
25	26	27	28	29	30	31

Wind swept sand dunes outside of Windorah, Queensland.
Photo: Paul Curtis.

Week 22

26 monday National Sorry Day

_____
_____
_____

27 tuesday ● Reconciliation Day (ACT)

_____
_____
_____

28 wednesday

_____
_____
_____

29 thursday

_____
_____
_____

30 friday

_____
_____
_____

31 saturday

_____
_____
_____

1 sunday

_____
_____

JUNE

S	M	T	W	T	F	S
1	2	3	4	5	6	7
8	9	10	11	12	13	14
15	16	17	18	19	20	21
22	23	24	25	26	27	28
29	30					

Frozen alpine tarns at the Pools of Bethesda,
Walls of Jerusalem National Park, Tasmania.

Week 23

June

2 monday   Western Australia Day (WA), Reconciliation Day Holiday (ACT)

3 tuesday ◐

4 wednesday

5 thursday

6 friday

7 saturday

8 sunday

JUNE

S	M	T	W	T	F	S
1	2	3	4	5	6	7
8	9	10	11	12	13	14
15	16	17	18	19	20	21
22	23	24	25	26	27	28
29	30					

Australian sea-lions *(Neophoca cinerea)*, Seal Bay Aquatic Reserve,
Kangaroo Island, South Australia.

Week 24

9 monday   King's Birthday (except Qld & WA)

10 tuesday

11 wednesday ○

12 thursday

13 friday

14 saturday

15 sunday

JUNE						
S	M	T	W	T	F	S
1	2	3	4	5	6	7
8	9	10	11	12	13	14
15	16	17	18	19	20	21
22	23	24	25	26	27	28
29	30					

Icicles near The Cathedral, Mount Buffalo National Park,
Victoria.

June

16 monday

17 tuesday

18 wednesday

19 thursday ◑

20 friday

21 saturday

22 sunday

JUNE

S	M	T	W	T	F	S
1	2	3	4	5	6	7
8	9	10	11	12	13	14
15	16	17	18	19	20	21
22	23	24	25	26	27	28
29	30					

Limestone karst rock formations at Chillagoe-Mungana Caves
National Park, Queensland.

Week 26

June

23 monday

24 tuesday

25 wednesday ●

26 thursday

27 friday

28 saturday

29 sunday

JUNE

S	M	T	W	T	F	S
1	2	3	4	5	6	7
8	9	10	11	12	13	14
15	16	17	18	19	20	21
22	23	24	25	26	27	28
29	30					

Emerging from rising mist The Cathedral stands high within
Mount Buffalo National Park, Victoria.

Week 27

30 monday

1 tuesday

2 wednesday

3 thursday ◗

4 friday

5 saturday

6 sunday

JULY

S	M	T	W	T	F	S
		1	2	3	4	5
6	7	8	9	10	11	12
13	14	15	16	17	18	19
20	21	22	23	24	25	26
27	28	29	30	31		

Mobs of emu *(Dromaius novaehollandia)* roaming across
Kangaroo Hills Station, Queensland.

Week 28

7 monday
_____
_____
_____

8 tuesday
_____
_____
_____

9 wednesday
_____
_____
_____

10 thursday
_____
_____
_____

11 friday ○
_____
_____
_____

12 saturday
_____
_____
_____

13 sunday
_____
_____

JULY						
S	M	T	W	T	F	S
		1	2	3	4	5
6	7	8	9	10	11	12
13	14	15	16	17	18	19
20	21	22	23	24	25	26
27	28	29	30	31		

Flowering pink mulla mulla (Ptilotis exaltatus),
Channel Country, Queensland.
Photo: Paul Curtis.

Week 29

14 monday

15 tuesday

16 wednesday

17 thursday

18 friday ◑

19 saturday

20 sunday

			JULY			
S	M	T	W	T	F	S
		1	2	3	4	5
6	7	8	9	10	11	12
13	14	15	16	17	18	19
20	21	22	23	24	25	26
27	28	29	30	31		

A male Great bowerbird *(Chlamydera nuchalis)* tending to his bower,
Kakadu National Park, Northern Territory.
Photo: Stanley Breeden.

Week 30

21 monday

22 tuesday

23 wednesday

24 thursday

25 friday ●

26 saturday

27 sunday

JULY

S	M	T	W	T	F	S
		1	2	3	4	5
6	7	8	9	10	11	12
13	14	15	16	17	18	19
20	21	22	23	24	25	26
27	28	29	30	31		

Polished stone near Rookwood Crossing, Walsh River,
Queensland.

Week 31

28 monday

29 tuesday

30 wednesday

31 thursday

1 friday ◑

2 saturday

3 sunday

AUGUST						
S	M	T	W	T	F	S
31					1	2
3	4	5	6	7	8	9
10	11	12	13	14	15	16
17	18	19	20	21	22	23
24	25	26	27	28	29	30

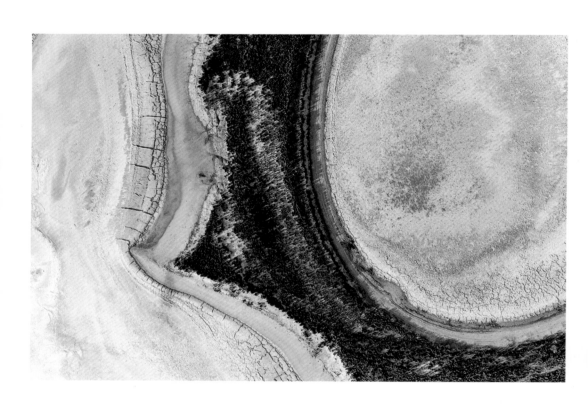

A small detail of the vast salt lakes near Jam Patch Nature Reserve,
Western Australia.

Week 32

4 monday   Picnic Day (NT)

5 tuesday

6 wednesday

7 thursday

8 friday

9 saturday ○

10 sunday

S	M	T	W	T	F	S
31					1	2
3	4	5	6	7	8	9
10	11	12	13	14	15	16
17	18	19	20	21	22	23
24	25	26	27	28	29	30

A light dusting of snow across Mount Buffalo National Park, Victoria.

Week 33

11 monday

12 tuesday

13 wednesday   Brisbane Show Day (Qld)

14 thursday

15 friday

16 saturday ◑

17 sunday

AUGUST

S	M	T	W	T	F	S
31					1	2
3	4	5	6	7	8	9
10	11	12	13	14	15	16
17	18	19	20	21	22	23
24	25	26	27	28	29	30

Little red flying-foxes *(Pteropus scapulatus)* being harassed
by a raptor above, Duaringa, Queensland.

Week 34

18 monday

19 tuesday

20 wednesday

21 thursday

22 friday

23 saturday ●

24 sunday

AUGUST

S	M	T	W	T	F	S
31					1	2
3	4	5	6	7	8	9
10	11	12	13	14	15	16
17	18	19	20	21	22	23
24	25	26	27	28	29	30

Moody light on Thistle Cove, Cape Le Grand National Park,
Western Australia.

Week 35

25 monday

26 tuesday

27 wednesday

28 thursday

29 friday

30 saturday

31 sunday

AUGUST

S	M	T	W	T	F	S
31					1	2
3	4	5	6	7	8	9
10	11	12	13	14	15	16
17	18	19	20	21	22	23
24	25	26	27	28	29	30

Swirling creek waters plunge into the Tully Gorge,
Tully Gorge National Park, Queensland.

Week 36

September

1 monday

2 tuesday

3 wednesday

4 thursday

5 friday

6 saturday

7 sunday   Father's Day

SEPTEMBER

S	M	T	W	T	F	S
		1	2	3	4	5	6
7	8	9	10	11	12	13
14	15	16	17	18	19	20
21	22	23	24	25	26	27
28	29	30				

Looking down over the Arthur River from Sumac Lookout,
Tarkine wilderness, Tasmania.

Week 37

September

8   monday ○

9   tuesday

10   wednesday

11   thursday

12   friday

13   saturday

14   sunday ◑

SEPTEMBER

S	M	T	W	T	F	S
		1	2	3	4	5	6
7	8	9	10	11	12	13
14	15	16	17	18	19	20
21	22	23	24	25	26	27
28	29	30				

Salt encrusted Lake Grace, Western Australia.

Week 38

September

15 monday

16 tuesday

17 wednesday

18 thursday

19 friday

20 saturday

21 sunday

SEPTEMBER						
S	M	T	W	T	F	S
		1	2	3	4	5	6
7	8	9	10	11	12	13
14	15	16	17	18	19	20
21	22	23	24	25	26	27
28	29	30				

Female wallaroo *(Macropus robustus)*, Kakadu National Park,
Northern Territory.
Photo: Stanley Breeden.

Week 39

22 monday ●

---

23 tuesday

---

24 wednesday

---

25 thursday

---

26 friday

---

27 saturday

---

28 sunday

SEPTEMBER

S	M	T	W	T	F	S
	1	2	3	4	5	6
7	8	9	10	11	12	13
14	15	16	17	18	19	20
21	22	23	24	25	26	27
28	29	30				

Brown falcons *(Falco berigora)* circle over fire searching for
flushed prey in Kakadu National Park, Northern Territory.
Photo: Stanley Breeden.

Week 40

September / October

29 monday   King's Birthday (WA)

30 tuesday ◑

1 wednesday

2 thursday

3 friday

4 saturday

5 sunday

S	M	T	W	T	F	S
			1	2	3	4
5	6	7	8	9	10	11
12	13	14	15	16	17	18
19	20	21	22	23	24	25
26	27	28	29	30	31	

Exposed granite rock coastline of Waychinicup National Park, Western Australia.

Week 41

6 monday King's Birthday (Qld), Labour Day (ACT, NSW & SA)

7 tuesday ○

8 wednesday

9 thursday

10 friday

11 saturday

12 sunday

OCTOBER

S	M	T	W	T	F	S
			1	2	3	4
5	6	7	8	9	10	11
12	13	14	15	16	17	18
19	20	21	22	23	24	25
26	27	28	29	30	31	

Backlit detail of a Spotted gum *(Corymbia citriodora)*,
Blackdown Tableland National Park, Queensland.

Week 42

October

13 monday

14 tuesday ◐

15 wednesday

16 thursday

17 friday

18 saturday

19 sunday

OCTOBER

S	M	T	W	T	F	S
			1	2	3	4
5	6	7	8	9	10	11
12	13	14	15	16	17	18
19	20	21	22	23	24	25
26	27	28	29	30	31	

Elephant Rocks and Greens Pool, William Bay National Park,
Western Australia.

Week 43

20 monday

21 tuesday ⬤

22 wednesday

23 thursday Royal Hobart Show Day (Tas)

24 friday

25 saturday

26 sunday

OCTOBER

S	M	T	W	T	F	S
			1	2	3	4
5	6	7	8	9	10	11
12	13	14	15	16	17	18
19	20	21	22	23	24	25
26	27	28	29	30	31	

A timeworn river red gum *(Eucalyptus camaldulensis)*
before the eastern face of Wilpena Pound,
Ikara-Flinders Ranges National Park, South Australia.

Week 44

October / November

27 monday

28 tuesday

29 wednesday

30 thursday ◑

31 friday

1 saturday

2 sunday

			NOVEMBER			
S	M	T	W	T	F	S
30						1
2	3	4	5	6	7	8
9	10	11	12	13	14	15
16	17	18	19	20	21	22
23	24	25	26	27	28	29

Lumholtz's tree-kangaroo *(Dendrolagus lumholtzi)*
moving about in daylight near Malanda, Queensland.

Week 45

3 monday   Recreation Day (Tas)

4 tuesday   Melbourne Cup Day (Vic)

5 wednesday

6 thursday ○

7 friday

8 saturday

9 sunday

NOVEMBER

S	M	T	W	T	F	S
30						1
2	3	4	5	6	7	8
9	10	11	12	13	14	15
16	17	18	19	20	21	22
23	24	25	26	27	28	29

Morning mist floating through the Grose Valley,
Blue Mountains National Park, New South Wales.

Week 46

10 monday

11 tuesday   Remembrance Day

12 wednesday ◑

13 thursday

14 friday

15 saturday

16 sunday

NOVEMBER

S	M	T	W	T	F	S
30						1
2	3	4	5	6	7	8
9	10	11	12	13	14	15
16	17	18	19	20	21	22
23	24	25	26	27	28	29

The unique grass tree *(Kingia australis)* is endemic to
Waychinicup National Park, Western Australia.

Week 47

17 monday

18 tuesday

19 wednesday

20 thursday ●

21 friday

22 saturday

23 sunday

NOVEMBER						
S	M	T	W	T	F	S
30						1
2	3	4	5	6	7	8
9	10	11	12	13	14	15
16	17	18	19	20	21	22
23	24	25	26	27	28	29

Folded and faulted mountain range,
Ikara-Flinders Ranges National Park, South Australia.

Week 48

24 monday

25 tuesday

26 wednesday

27 thursday

28 friday ◐

29 saturday

30 sunday

NOVEMBER

S	M	T	W	T	F	S
30						1
2	3	4	5	6	7	8
9	10	11	12	13	14	15
16	17	18	19	20	21	22
23	24	25	26	27	28	29

Noisy friarbirds *(Philemon corniculatus)* feasting on the nectar
of the flowering *Xanthorrhoea* and the insects it attracts,
Mount Spurgeon National Park, Queensland.

Week 49

December

1 monday

2 tuesday

3 wednesday

4 thursday

5 friday ○

6 saturday

7 sunday

DECEMBER

S	M	T	W	T	F	S
	1	2	3	4	5	6
7	8	9	10	11	12	13
14	15	16	17	18	19	20
21	22	23	24	25	26	27
28	29	30	31			

Cauliflorous fig, Wooroonooran National Park, Queensland.

8 monday

9 tuesday

10 wednesday

11 thursday

12 friday ◐

13 saturday

14 sunday

DECEMBER

S	M	T	W	T	F	S
	1	2	3	4	5	6
7	8	9	10	11	12	13
14	15	16	17	18	19	20
21	22	23	24	25	26	27
28	29	30	31			

Silhouette of Royal Spoonbills *(Platalea regia)*,
Townsville Town Common Conservation Park, Queensland.

Week 51

December

15 monday

16 tuesday

17 wednesday

18 thursday

19 friday

20 saturday ●

21 sunday

DECEMBER

S	M	T	W	T	F	S
		1	2	3	4	5	6
7	8	9	10	11	12	13
14	15	16	17	18	19	20
21	22	23	24	25	26	27
28	29	30	31			

Backlight illuminating the flowers of a bridal tree *(Xanthostemon paradoxus)*, Kakadu National Park, Northern Territory, Australia. Photo: Stanley Breeden.

Week 52

22 monday

23 tuesday

24 wednesday

25 thursday   Christmas Day

26 friday   Boxing Day

27 saturday

28 sunday ◑

DECEMBER						
S	M	T	W	T	F	S
		1	2	3	4	5	6
7	8	9	10	11	12	13
14	15	16	17	18	19	20
21	22	23	24	25	26	27
28	29	30	31			

Beauchamp Falls, Great Otway National Park, Victoria.

Week 53

December / January

29 monday

30 tuesday

31 wednesday

1 thursday New Year's Day

2 friday

3 saturday ○

4 sunday

JANUARY 2026

S	M	T	W	T	F	S
				1	2	3
4	5	6	7	8	9	10
11	12	13	14	15	16	17
18	19	20	21	22	23	24
25	26	27	28	29	30	31

River red gums stand guard at Ikara-Flinders Ranges National Park, South Australia.

Names & Addresses

A

B

C

D

E

F

G

H

I

J

Names & Addresses

K

L

M

N

O

P

Q

R

S

T

U

V

W

X

Y

Z

Notes